MW01705155

Always bear in mind that your own resolution to succeed is more important than any other.

Abraham Lincoln

Twelve Guaranteed Ways To Stay Miserable, Or Not…

(Secrets to Eliminating Depression, Anxiety and Other Emotional Pitfalls)

Mini-Memory Jogger

By Patricia L. Zerman, MS, LPC

Twelve Guaranteed Ways To Stay Miserable, Or Not…

(Secrets to Eliminating Depression, Anxiety and Other Emotional Pitfalls)
Mini-Memory Jogger

Published by Atlanta Awareness Center Publishing
www.AtlantaAwarenessCenter.com
1373 Old Virginia Court, SE
Marietta, GA 30067 (770-953-3136)

ISBN: 978-1-61005-130-9

First Printing - November, 2010
Cover Design by Publication Services
Illustrations by H.C. Clements
Graphic Design by Rick Presley and Roger Koo
Edited by Pam Ryan and Beverly Wolf
Design Specialist Robert Swanson

Table of Contents

R

Introduction

This mini reference book is to help jog your memory. We all slip from time to time and this handy reminder will keep you on your toes. Life is a journey, and staying focused is important. I lovingly present to you the ups and downs, curses and blessings of we who are commonly known in today's jargon as "seekers".

You will find this short guide presents a step ladder (the "how to's") of inner investigation that quiets the mind-chatter, leading you to a place of silence that allows you to hear that still small voice.

Your natural being is not in the becoming process. When you are convinced of this it brings a new dimension to living, an opening that is beyond all becoming. You can never obtain what you are. It reveals itself by itself. Enjoy!

Faith is taking the first step when you don’t see the whole staircase.

Martin Luther King, Jr.

Next Exit Misery

Rutgar is a detective, a great detective! He's been a natural born snoop all his life. It's no wonder he grew up to be a well-respected and much sought-after private investigator.

He cannot stop wondering why people do the crazy things they do and is continuously amazed by the antics of their repeated messes.

"Rocky, if people only believed they were valuable enough to face their problems, follow their intuition and speak up, I'd be out of a job in no time," he laughed as he spoke to his trusty four-legged companion.

So it's no wonder with all the hoopla he heard about a place called Misery, he felt compelled to investigate. My intuition tells me that something is not right, and my intuition has never failed.

The perplexing thing about Misery is that so many people live there. They all say they want to leave, but rarely do. "Why is that?"

Misery Rules and Regulations Sign

Arriving in Misery was a shock! They had no idea what they were going to find but were prepared for the worst.

After all, nothing good had ever been said about this place. One thing he knew for sure, Misery had a reputation as an awful place to live.

Rutgar immediately got a creepy feeling in the pit of his stomach. The situation was worse than he suspected. Nobody smiled.

Everyone seemed to be on edge and suspicious, as if they had the weight of the world on their shoulders.

As his eyes roamed the site he couldn't help but notice a huge sign at Misery's entrance. No one could miss this! Rutgar's faced turned ashen as he read it.

Rocky buried his head under his paws after seeing the expression on his master's face. Rutgar gasped as he studied the words:

Never Be Selfish

(Rule 1)

In Misery we encourage people to walk all over each other. It's necessary to give up your personal interests for the sake of others to live in Misery.

Simply put, you never come first. Your wants and needs don't count. You're not important. To assist with memorizing this rule, it's helpful to use the analogy of being a doormat.

Never follow your intuition either. Ignore its direction and argue and fight those dastardly tugs in your tummy. Don't forget to say "yes" when you mean "no" and "no" when you mean "yes".

This helps you lose sight of who you are by encouraging you to continuously go against your needs and desires.

We want to enforce uniformity in Misery, that's why we've adopted "Misery Loves Company" as our town motto.

Join the crowd by not rocking the boat and it's certain you'll help keep misery alive and well.

Avoid and Pretend

(Rule 2)

This is a sure-fire way to max out emotionally and make your stay in Misery more perplexing.

Avoid and ignore all emotions that make you feel crazy and sick inside by pretending that everything is okay when it isn't.

It sort of feels like not studying for an upcoming test or keeping your mouth shut when you want to scream, according to most residents.

You'll find these two types of denial make it easy to live in Misery by causing loads of frustration and irritation, not to mention ulcers. It gets better.

Depression is one of the grander returns accompanying this method of coping. Repeatedly denying true feelings propels agony to new heights. How do you think you found this place?

Keep pretending no one can see you while your head is stuck in the sand and brace yourself for a swift kick from behind. The Ostrich Syndrome has much to offer with assisting you in perfecting this rule.

Live In Fear

(Rule 3)

A great way to live miserably is to be controlled by fear. Refuse to confront uncomfortable situations head on.

Count on endless suffering by running away from what scares you. Fear gains more power becoming quite insurmountable and even bigger when you don't. And we all know, bigger is better!

The thing that makes fear so much fun is that it's self-manufactured, meaning you do this to yourself. So take the time to be imaginative, this way you can dream up so many unrealistic fears you're too scared to make a move.

Fear's intensity magnifies each time it's rehashed. Recollecting the bits and pieces puts them back together again.

Make sure to beat yourself up by creating scarier revisions. Keep past worries and reactions close at hand.

What a grand scheme for creating frightful scenarios!

Lie to Yourself and Others

(Rule 4)

Liars are welcomed and encouraged in Misery. Be certain you join them. Lying quadruples worthlessness, a highly sought-after result here.

You've lied to yourself enough over the years. It's time to share the fun! Like wildfire, lies destructively spread and build on themselves.

It's best to start with little white lies and work up to the big whoppers. You have lied over the years, so you know the drill.

That's what living in Misery is all about. No doubt, the constant upheaval keeps you walking on eggshells.

There's an additional perk, trying not to forget the lies already told! It's very exhilarating and leads to loads of anxiety.

It's fun to see residents squirm from getting caught up in the layers of lies. We do not value trust in Misery and find it offensive when people speak truthfully.

React and Become Defensive

(Rule 5)

Do you like living life as one big sore spot? Becoming one of the walking wounded instills touchiness beyond belief and has its own rewards.

When offered any form of constructive criticism, be reactionary. Make sure to lash out at others for the emotional wounds you carry.

Don't bother listening to or digesting what people say to you either.

When you feel raw and upset, rather than discovering why words or actions knock up against you, become numb and feel damaged. Stay puffed up, brittle, and sore. Sulking and pouting are beneficial, too!

There's nothing more miserable than walking around like a huge dart board. No doubt, you will fit right in with our crowd.

Keeping a scowl on your face also helps. We offer scowl-training classes for those who have not perfected the "right look" and free access to Lake Woe-Is-Me to bask in touchiness.

Rationalize, Analyze, and Stuff

(Rule 6)

Dwelling on trials and tribulations captivates the mind by redirecting and diverting emotions. This makes you look like you are really smart.

You appear to have an intellectual advantage. Since you can't think and feel at the same time, rationalizing and analyzing allow you to temporarily reroute what's actually going on.

We are well aware that thinking profoundly multiples problems. It's a wolf in sheep's clothing, exactly how misery thrives and stays alive.

Stuffing problems by rationalizing and analyzing them to death helps produce anxiety, pressure and stress. Add constant agitation into the mix as well. Tossing and turning on your agenda?

Forget embracing emotions. The resulting tension will build up and like a volcano you'll eventually explode. This is the ticket to that long-awaited nervous breakdown you have anticipated for years.

One Finger Out

(Rule 7)

This is a little trick that keeps you from taking any responsibility, a terrific way to escape reality and be terminally dependent on blame.

As long as you are convinced that the root cause of any problem is somebody else, moving out of Misery is not an option. This is what you're really hoping for, isn't it?

If you work at total abdication of ownership for everything, you can develop an amazing ability to justify why it's always someone else's fault.

Refusing to be held accountable is a marvelous way to drag out suffering for eons and also why finger pointing is a featured talent of our residents.

To maintain your status in Misery and uphold the covenants properly, we ask that you follow this rule carefully.

It's mandatory that you keep that index finger armed, cocked, and ready to point at anyone but yourself.

Manipulate and Have Motives

(Rule 8)

Tired of not getting what you want? Join the club! In Misery we pride ourselves on taking charge of our destinies through manipulation.

When you aren't getting what you desire, manipulation is a viable solution to your dilemma. You want results now!

Unless you manipulate the situation, you're afraid you'll never get your reward. Have it your way! That's the spirit we like here.

It's more stimulating anyway. Manipulating yourself and others to circumvent the truth isn't honest and keeps you perpetually scurrying.

Make manipulation a priority. Top it off by throwing in loads of motives as well. It's a significant part of sustaining a high-quality life in Misery.

Of course, that's the point right? You never know, you might become famous. You're familiar with soap opera and reality shows. First rate drama comes from manipulation loaded with motives. One of our TV scouts might be around the corner.

Swim in Guilt

(Rule 9)

This rule requires little or no explanation. Where would Misery be without guilt?

How would we know how to discipline our children, let alone ourselves, if it weren't for guilt? Guilt destroys many lives.

It is subtle and generally goes undetected for years and feels more like a mild annoyance than the destroyer it is. It's a favorite rule, one of Misery's most popular.

Whether you are trying to control yourself or someone else is working hard to control you, there are lots of should haves, could haves, or ought to's involved.

Those heavy, ingrained feelings of duty, obligation, and responsibility build relentlessly — perfect for sustaining misery.

They become ominous foreboding emotions, sort of like waiting for a tornado to touch down. Guilt's aftermath leaves parts of you scattered everywhere. If being locked in depression is a life-long dream guilt is the perfect nightmare to make it come true.

Anger, Resentment, and Blame

(Rule 10)

Do you dream of aspiring to everlasting victim-hood? One powerful way to absolutely ruin your life is to hang onto anger and resentment.

Make sure to blame everyone in your life but you for what's happened. OF COURSE, it's not your fault.

How you live is definitely based on the others around you, especially your uncaring boss, insensitive friends and unfeeling spouse.

Not getting what you want isn't a shortcoming of yours by any means. If it doesn't work, it must have something to do with outside forces, not self-imposed limitations.

There's no better reward than having a tantrum, stomping your feet and throwing a fit! We support this behavior by inviting you to our annual Bellowing Ball.

This Grand Gala offers the opportunity to justify rage by projecting all the damage you've experienced onto others.

Worry

(Rule 11)

Worry is a fabulous way to stay immobilized in Misery. You get to feel paranoid, live in constant fear and continually experience life as a perpetual guessing game.

Worrying keeps you removed from yourself, diverting discomfort by endlessly picking things apart.

This offers a false sense of control and is acceptable as a first line of defense. But in truth, worry is only a way to con yourself into believing you can ditch fear of the unknown by thinking things to death.

It's a dramatic mind trick assured to draw attention straight to insecurities, doubts, and fears. Your pronouncement of good/bad or right/wrong actually makes you believe your senseless judgment has relevance.

Feeling trapped in a never-ending time warp of worry's paranoia is like living in a made-to-order haunted house. There is no end to the suffering. Join the "What If" league too. They meet weekly to practice projection.

Don't Risk

(Rule 12)

Can't stand anything new? Don't like things out of the ordinary? We proudly promote procrastination! Don't risk, that way you won't feel threatened, and isn't that the reason you were attracted to Misery?

Not risking is indisputably and unquestionably a lack-luster way to stay miserable. There's no need to worry about ever feeling disoriented or facing what's new and frightening.

If living in a rut is your heart's desire, you've finally found something that leads to satisfaction. You are free to live an uninspired, dreary, mundane existence forever. Try new things? Hogwash! Act like a possum and play dead.

Not risking leaves you wondering why you are here. Miserable and melancholy sum it up. Let this be your slogan, "If I don't risk, I won't exist."

Not risking change allows you to procrastinate as long as you like, bringing life to a virtual halt. It creates a life of mediocrity. What more could you ask for?

Surrender To Helplessness

Summary of Rules and Regulations For Living In Misery

Surrender To Helplessness And Become Hopeless

If the *Twelve Guaranteed Ways to Stay Miserable* have not created a clear picture of what you are required to do to live in Misery, then we suggest our final option, "Surrender to Helplessness and Become Hopeless".

This option includes the others but takes living in Misery a step further. Noted to be destructive, it's the best way to take living in Misery to another level. When all else fails, simply give up on life. This option affords the ability to feel sorry for yourself, to justify your plight. "Poor me" sums it up perfectly. Using this formula it's impossible to remove yourself from the rut of self-condemnation.

We in Misery have discovered that it is a whole lot easier to throw in the towel than to accept responsibility. It's too logical to ask for help. Forget doing a little digging inside to see where self-defeat and worthlessness began. We don't want to be freed from the trap we're in.

Instead, stay cemented in self-pity, dropping into a bottomless sinkhole of depression. At this stage we never accept there is a way out.

Life is a series of experiences, each one of which makes us bigger, even though sometimes it is hard to realize this.

Henry Ford

Had Enough Misery?

Rutgar was dumfounded by what he read in Misery's Rules & Regulations. He flung the Welcome Kit into the back seat.

"Why in the world would anyone want to live that way?" he said out loud. He didn't mind asking for help when necessary. "Why suffer?"

He was amused that people struggle with change. In a world that is temporary people seek permanence. Change is a constant fact of human existence.

In his own life he'd come to see the chaos and disruption created from transition taught him the most. That is, when he was willing to let himself be open and work it through.

Life isn't as hard as people believe. It's a shame they won't doubt their self-imposed persecution. He realized that when the dust settled a surprising gift was left behind. It wasn't easy to ride stuff out, but he was certain his solution was much better than living in Misery.

What is there to lose?

Leaving Misery Behind

(New Rules & Regulations)

Official Welcome Kit

Rules & Regulations For Living In Misery

Compliance Mandatory

As he stared out at Misery's landscape, Rutgar reflected on the number of times he had felt crappy throughout his life. It was uncomfortable.

"I am not meant to live in Misery. Every time I'm down in the dumps I eventually reach a point where I am just 'sick and tired of being sick and tired'."

"It has taken incredible dedication, commitment and determination to get myself out of the emotional potholes I've fallen into. Yet, I've never regretted it. The inhabitants of Misery need shaking up! Ha, *Twelve Guaranteed Ways To Stay Miserable*, what a crock!"

Rutgar had an idea. He would override Misery's Mayor and City Council and rewrite the Rules & Regulations, calling it *Twelve Guaranteed Ways To Leave Misery Behind*.

"When I'm finished," he deviously smirked looking at Rocky, "you and I will sneak back into Misery's Welcome Center and replace their kits with ours. A clandestine scheme and freedom-seekers dream!"

Be Selfish With A Capital "S"

(New Rule 1)

Learn to put yourself first in every decision you make. Like it or not, you will come to understand that you are number one. You are all you've got!

Simply put, you must come first. Your wants and needs count. You matter. To remember this rule, think about the phrase Selfishness with a Capital "S". That means nothing or no one is more important than you are. Without you there IS nothing else.

Caring for you is paramount to lasting happiness. Putting other people first (sacrifice dolled up as exemplary behavior) is backwards. You end up keeping score, holding grudges and bitter. It's dishonest.

Being Selfish with a capital "S" means admitting the soul-based truth about how you feel and honoring it, never going against your tummy (that gut feeling that nudges at you twenty-four hours a day). It's a permanent solution without hidden agendas; the highest level of living where trust abounds and everyone wins!

Refuse to Avoid and Pretend, Act

(New Rule 2)

Avoiding and pretending are skills picked up over the years; for some it's an art.

Both are resourceful techniques for overlooking matters you don't want to deal with.

They allow you to believe you're okay when you're not.

Avoidance rears its head in many forms. Excessive exercise, under or overeating, drinking too much, taking drugs, cutting, being a workaholic, addictive sex, gambling and overspending are examples.

These are diversions used to anesthetize so you don't feel what desperately needs to be felt, ways to fill the void left from ignoring what's going on inside.

Face apprehension instead. Self-reliance breeds the security, confidence, and independence necessary to have faith in you. Don't stop reaching.

"The longest journey ever taken is the eighteen inches from your head to your heart." Why wait?

Face Fear

(New Rule 3)

You know what fear feels like. Remember that time you were shaken by a near-miss collision or took a test without studying? The times when you couldn't calm the butterflies and nervous energy while waiting for a life-altering phone call?

Or when you felt rejected by a lover and never discussed it? Each situation was overshadowed with fearful flashes of uncertainty. "The only way out is through."

Dissolve the judgment that paralyzes potential. Allow common sense to rule. Put an end to fearful thoughts that are filtered through worry. Clear out the anxiety causing you to see distorted images. Take control.

Have the courage to face what you don't want to see. Practice by using your mind to walk through threatening mental pictures. Like seeing a movie again and again, fear-filled scenarios will lose their punch.

Fear is nothing more than False Expectations Appearing Real. Dare to challenge mental images and be free!

Liars Lose

(New Rule 4)

Do you lie? Fess up. Tell the truth, if to no one but yourself. What about the little white lies you consider harmless?

The ones you tell to spare your feelings or someone else's. If you're one of many, let it be said in no uncertain terms that the world mirrors those lies back to you.

The way you treat others is exactly how you assume they are going to treat you! Wonder why you don't trust anyone and assume people are out to get you? You are not here to live dishonestly.

Ask yourself why you believe you are unworthy to tell the truth. Why you are responsible for protecting another's feelings? You don't have to be mean, simply come from integrity and respect. Children do it and we love them for it.

Stop being dishonest, it makes everyone suspicious. Try being genuine and real and watch how safe you feel. If you want to make the world a better place, start by telling the truth. The reward surpasses the risk!

Defy Defensiveness

(New Rule 5)

Touchiness is a blatant symptom of little or no self-worth. Being sensitive means you think another's point of view is more important than yours and you are looking for approval.

You refuse to be seen as a peer and this is what makes you angry. Rather than standing up for yourself, you act out by becoming belligerent, guarded or quarrelsome, fueling the mounting upset.

To top it off, your defensiveness makes communication very difficult. One slip of the tongue and you act destroyed. You can't ignore what's bothering you. It won't disappear into thin air.

Defy defensiveness and resist reaction. When something bumps up against you, own it. Do a U-turn and admit what sets you off. Realize that it's a gift in disguise. Start appreciating irritation and rejection.

Pain is the amount of love you withhold from yourself. It points toward unhealed wounds, a trigger. "It's not out there." Find out why!

Resist Rationalizing, Analyzing and Stuffing

(New Rule 6)

Thinking isn't feeling and feeling is an important tool in life. Thinking is stuffing, not experiencing or savoring feelings separates us from computers, without them you are nothing more than a robot.

When you use mental software to decipher what is happening emotionally or pick things apart in minute detail you lock-up. Eventually you have to reboot. Operating correctly, feelings act as indicators or alarms that something is being set off inside.

When it's time to act they scream out, but all too often you don't listen to them. You've inadvertently trained yourself to follow your intellect instead of addressing feelings.

Rationalizing, analyzing or stuffing are all non-emotional and only appear to be viable ways to escape uncomfortable feelings. If you knew the far-reaching consequences, you'd quit.

Experience feelings — ironically, allowing what bubbles up makes it dissolve and disappear. It's that simple: Dive in and swim in your emotions!

Pause Instead of Point

(New Rule 7)

Blaming others is a temporary fix. Pointing a finger seems like a short cut, a clever distraction to avert ownership, a grand deflection.

It's not, no matter how justified your plight seems to be. Instead of offering freedom, projection acts as a reflection of your denial. What you avoid internally ends up controlling your actions.

These repressed emotions affect everything that crosses your path. You wouldn't be using that finger unless something is getting a little too close for comfort.

It doesn't matter if predicaments are large or small; the bottom line is that something is eating at you. Project means "to throw out or hurl away from or toward something else". It's a sneaky way to redirect responsibility outside you and leave it there. The term "scapegoat" aptly describes this function.

Here is the solution: Who is the one seeing it, feeling it and hearing it? Since the answer is always "Me" guess who has work to do?

Marginalize Motive and Manipulation

(New Rule 8)

Whether it's overt or inconspicuously subtle, manipulation never pans out. It is a modified version of dishonesty, which is a form of deceit and underhanded scheming to get what you want. Sly and devious sum it up.

The reality of the situation isn't providing the desired outcome, so you fall back on manipulation as a means to an end or allow yourself to be manipulated into something.

The truth isn't suitable, "Taking things into your own hands" appears be more satisfactory. You want to be in charge.

Calculated thinking provides evidence that there's an underlying motive. That's what lets you know there is a problem. Manipulation offers a false sense of hope.

But that false sense of hope never delivers, like a drug. To the addict, it makes things tolerable. Do you want relief? Drop hope. Quit thinking you know the answer and be patient. Your limited thinking, plotting and planning are the problem. If it were meant to pan out, don't you think it would on its own?

Trade Guilt for Gratitude

(New Rule 9)

Everybody has felt guilty at some point. Guilt arises when you set aside feelings, not accepting and acknowledging your truth, then acting on it.

By refusing to tell it like it is and swallowing personal pride you take a back seat. Real feelings are stuffed in the guise of protecting. You prefer to be seen as "good," instead of being truthful.

Not wanting to make waves is an inner code of ethics that dictates, "I'll sacrifice me for you." Unwritten rules teach you to repress rising anger and train you to believe it's not valid. Be grateful and pay attention.

Guilt is defined as, "Anger I'm afraid I'll get into trouble for," and has been termed the *Silent Destroyer*. It's a clue to freedom.

Instead of invaliding your feelings, be honest. Drop the burdens of the world. Let others take responsibility for their lives. Get rid of duty and obligation. Do things when you want to. Not because you have to. The world is beautiful when you cease being a martyr!

Applaud Anger, Resentment and Blame

(New Rule 10)

"Most people walk around like they are sitting on a powder keg and an insane man is holding a match." Anger, resentment, and blame are at a collective all-time high. It's always the other guy's fault, never yours.

As a general rule, somehow, someway there's somebody else to blame. It only takes seconds to conjure up rational explanations.

Don't step up to the plate and accept the mess you have allowed yourself to get into. This is a solid fact for everyone at some time in life. Say it isn't true.

The plight of mankind: the refusal to take responsibility. No matter how strongly you disagree, the fact is you are the only one that can fix what upsets you in life.

Whatever hooks you is precisely there to be healed no matter how distasteful. It happened, move forward. Stop blaming. There is one answer and one solution. Go look into a mirror. It is right before your eyes!

Wipe Out Worry

(New Rule 11)

Worry's magnetic hold doesn't miss a solitary soul. Even though it has no purpose other than to keep us tormented and miserable, we seem magically hypnotized by the incapacitating spells it casts.

Left on its own, it rapidly multiples like rabbits and is soon out of control. You drown helplessly in mental quicksand as it sucks you in.

How does something so utterly useless possess such astonishing power?

The ego is always blasting some form of "what isn't". Viciously taunting you, it argues constantly, determined to keep your emotions in an uproar.

Instead of taking a second to calm down and let the dust settle you seek immediate relief by stressing over every erroneous outcome you can dredge up.

You don't realize thinking pushes away solutions. Stop projecting. Stay NOW. Take deep breaths. Drop limitation and be willing not to know. There is always a next. Stay open!

Risk!

(New Rule 12)

"The only way out is through," is a significant phrase. Issues don't become etched in unless there's unfinished business. Predicaments of little concern are handled immediately, and then vanish. Nothing fearful maintains itself unless it's supported. Ironically, that's why it's there.

Typically, even if a situation is uncomfortable it beats trying something new, rocking the boat or possibly failing. Taking care of you ought to be the simplest task in the world. It's not.

In order to have new outcomes you must risk doing things differently. "Insanity is doing the same thing over and over again expecting different results." That is why risking is essential.

Each of us is responsible for dispelling the illusion of limitation. Taking risks is the key. See into the arbitrary limits that make you believe change is impossible.

"It is not death that a man should fear, but he should fear never beginning to live," Marcus Auerelius.

Take a chance!

Freedom

It was early morning when Rutgar and Rocky reached Misery. Today was the day!

The masked marauders were heading back to Misery to replace the old Welcome Kits with Rutgar's new and improved version.

Amazingly, the door to Misery's Welcome Center was unlocked. With Rocky in tow trembling, he rushed over to the desk where the Kits were stacked and made the exchange.

It took seconds to leap into the car and escape. "The perplexing thing about Misery is that too many people live there. They say they want to leave, but rarely do. Why?"

"Thank goodness the spell was broken. I woke up from the bad dream that held me captive. I refuse to accept the hypnotic suggestion that I must suffer. No one is meant to live in Misery."

As the sun rose, brilliant colors streaming from the first light of day touched them deeply. There is BOUNDLESS FREEDOM once Misery is left behind!

LEAVING
MISERY

The secret of happiness is freedom. The secret of freedom is courage.

Thucydides

About the Author

Armed with her heart and a compelling idea Patricia Zerman founded the Atlanta Awareness Center and has been providing dynamic personal and spiritual opportunities since 1989. Her true dedication has effectively transformed lives.

In order to help her survive personal challenges Pat discovered tools to get to the bottom of issues. Utilizing experience, a Master's Degree in Psychology and Georgia License she put a broad spectrum of material to the test. The answers she found provided welcome relief, guiding her to share this knowledge. The Center provides a specialized form of teaching, quickly getting to the root of problems. Clients learn to love and respect themselves by taking risks. Most people won't do this on their own.

They learn to get honest, stop avoiding and identify the conditioning that runs them. This enables rapid release of emotional blockage. Patricia helps clients practice practical skills, the "how to's," learning to live what self-help and therapy teach. These techniques allow individuals to live now, take responsibility, end blame, fully experience emotions, to forgive themselves and others. Most important, act independently, not through other people's opinions.

Pat's no-nonsense, action oriented approach mixes piercing discernment with forthright honesty, eliminating self-avoidance. This inspired clients to nickname her *The Laser Lady*. She shocks people by teaching them they must come first and why, stressing the term Selfishness with a Capital "S". Never sell yourself short. The results speak for themselves! If you want to experience independence through personal freedom visit: www.AtlantaAwarenessCenter.com or www.PatZerman.com or call 770-953-3136.

About the Illustrator

Huel Clement is an Atlanta, Georgia native. He served in the Gulf War, was an exemplary Cobb County policeman for ten years, and ironically a private detective. He is currently the Director of Security for a large hotel chain. His talents were discovered when he was only six years old. His father put artistic implements in front of him and he began to draw without prior training. The excitement wore off over the years because people took advantage of his skills and kind nature. Art became a burden.

When the idea of doing the illustrations for *Twelve Guaranteed Ways* came along, Huel was internally torn. Fortunately, he moved through the hesitation. Accepting the challenge opened up a closed off area within him and offered the freedom to embrace his remarkable talent once again, Huel continues to utilize this amazing creative outlet whenever there is time in his hectic schedule.

References and Resources

Books

Ramana Maharshi, *Be As You Are*, David Godman, Penguin Books, UK, 1989

John Bradshaw, *Heal The Shame That Binds You*, Health Communications, New York, New York, 2005

Susan Jeffers, PH.D., *Feel the Fear And Do It Anyway*, Ballentine Books, New York, New York, 2004

Joel S. Goldsmith, *Consciousness Transformed*, Acropolis Books Publishing, Lakewood, Colorado, 2002

Harvel Hendrix, PH.D., *Getting The Love You Want*, Holt-Henry Company, Gordonsville, Virginia, 2007

Gerald Jampolsky, MD, *Say Goodbye To Guilt, Love is Letting Go of Fear,* Center for Attitudinal Healing, Tiburon, California, 1985

Arnold M. Patent, *You Can Have It All*, Simon and Schuster, New York, New York, 1997

Watty Piper, *The Little Engine That Could*, Penguin-Putnam, New York, New York, 2002

William Samuel, *A Guide To Awareness and Tranquility*, William Samuel Foundation, Mountain Brook, Alabama, 2003

Eckhart Tolle, *Power of Now*, Namaste Publishing, Vancouver, B.C., 2004 Lying occurs when people desire to defend themselves or others. It's a form of insecurity.

Dr. Lawrence J. Peters, *Peter's Quotations*, Quill-Williams-Morrow, New York, New York, 1992

Classes

Susan Trout, PH.D., Institute for Attitudinal Studies, Alexandria, Virginia

Diane Cirincione, PH.D., Center For Attitudinal Healing, San Rafael, California

Kay Causey, *The Rest of Myself*, Adairsville, Georgia

Truth will ultimately prevail where there is pain to bring it to light.

George Washington

Twelve Guaranteed Ways To Stay Miserable, Or Not…

(Secrets to Eliminating Depression, Anxiety and Other Emotional Pitfalls)

Mini-Memory Jogger

To contact the author or order additional copies of
Twelve Guarantees to Stay Miserable or Not…, please mail correspondence to:

The Atlanta Awareness Center
Patricia Zerman, MS, LPC
1373 Old Virginia Court, SE
Marietta, GA 30067-8461

Or Online:
www.AtlantaAwarenessCenter.com (Website)
aac@AtlantaAwarenessCenter.com (Author's Direct Email)

Order Form

Name: ______________________________
Address: ______________________________
Phone: ______________________________
Email: ______________________________

	No. of Copies		Amount		Totals
Books:		x	**$9.95**		
Shipping:		x	**$2.95**	+	

Total Due: **$** ________ **US**

Please allow up to 3 weeks for delivery.